We Saw the Image of Jesus in the Clouds

Miracles

EDNA CASTRO

WestBow Press books may be ordered through booksellers or by contacting:

WestBow Press
A Division of Thomas Nelson & Zondervan
1663 Liberty Drive
Bloomington, IN 47403
www.westbowpress.com
1 (866) 928-1240

ISBN: 978-1-9736-7351-4 (sc)
ISBN: 978-1-9736-7352-1 (e)

Library of Congress Control Number: 2019912852

Print information available on the last page.

WestBow Press rev. date: 10/8/2019

WESTBOW
PRESS®
A DIVISION OF THOMAS NELSON
& ZONDERVAN

Contents

Preface

My name is Edna Castro (Vega). I was born May 14, 1954, at the Cumberland Hospital in Brooklyn, New York City. My parents were born in Puerto Rico. My mom's name is Luzvina Toro Vega. She was born on July 12, 1925, in Ponce, Puerto Rico. My dad's name is Luis E. Vega, he was born on April 10, in Yauco, Puerto Rico. Passed away in 1992. R.I.P. He had served our country in world war two.

My parents had ten children together. They got married and had my oldest brother who unfortunately died of natural causes when he was four months old (R.I.P.). The rest of my older siblings were born in Puerto Rico in the corresponding order: my oldest sister was born on March 10, 1948, my older brother was born on April 27, 1950, and just passed away 5-31-19. R.I.P. I was like his second mother to him, loved him dearly. And my other sister was born on March 1, 1952.

Shortly after, my family moved to Brooklyn, New York City, where I was born on May 14, 1954. I was the first of my siblings to be born in New York City. Two years later, there was another addition to the family my sister. She was born on July 7, 1956 when I was two years old. I remember my mom going into labor in her bedroom. Next thing I remember, our neighbors were coming into our house to help my mom. They were wonderful and stayed in the room with her. The door was open a little and I peeked into the room. Over the next few years, the rest of my brothers and sisters were born.

My brother was born on August 9, 1958. God bless him, he just beat stage 4 cancer Thank you God. My younger sister was born on March 5, 1959, and I lost her August 13, 2013 (R.I.P.) loved her dearly. My other sister was born August 5, 1960, and my youngest brother of the family, was born November 30, 1961.

Growing up with mom

From the day we were born my mom would take us to church every Sunday. I remember so long ago, using the beanie hats before entering mass all the time. As of today, most of my siblings and I still attend mass every Sunday. My mom doesn't attend mass because she can't walk now and has Alzheimer's, but they come from the church every Sunday to pray with her, she still knows how to pray and they give her Holy Communion.

1959
....

Started School

I started school in September 1959, I attended school at P.S. 298 in Brooklyn. After I graduated In September 1965, I proceeded to go to J.H.S. 263 in Brooklyn. While I was attending school in J.H.S. 263, my mother asked me, "do you want to go to Catholic School? I replied, ``Yes''. So she took me out of J.H.S. 263 in Brooklyn and registered me into Our Lady of Loretto School. I loved it there and meet lots of friends there. Eventually, she registered for the rest of my siblings to attend Our Lady of Loretto School also.

1968
....

In High School

At this time my mother had separated from my father and decided to move us to the Bronx. She raised all nine of us, all on her own. The only man she ever had was our father and never dated anyone else in her life again. Until 1992 before my father passed away, my mother and father reunited back together for several months then he passed away. R.I.P.

When I was younger, I was always looking forward to turning fourteen-years-old so that I could start working. I've always wanted to work. I got my first summer job at a summer youth program in 1968, and I was so happy that I had finally started to work. I loved that job because I got to work with children and I have always loved children. I had worked different jobs every summer break and always enjoyed working.

1971
· ·

I meet my fiance

When we moved to the Bronx, I met my boyfriend. He lived in one corner building, and I lived in the other corner building in the same block.

The first time we saw each other, he was playing handball against the wall, downstairs in the building that I lived in. This was during his lunch break while working. As he was playing handball, I asked him, "Who has next? He replied. "You do" and after he finished his game, he gave me the ball and left back to work.

In September 1971, after seeing him outside several times, I noticed he was following me around in his brother-in-laws car with his family and friends.

One day he saw my sister and told her that he wanted to speak to me. So my sister told me and I went upstairs to meet with him. Then he spoke to me and he asked me to be his girlfriend. I replied, "Only if you don't have a girlfriend". He replied, ``No I don't." So we started to date.

While we dated, I got to see him when he came to my house which was almost every day. We were very much in love. My mom was very strict and never left me out of the house to go anywhere but to school. When my boyfriend came to visit me at my house, my mom would sit in between the living room and the kitchen to watch us. Then at 8:30 pm she would turn off the lights so that he would go home.

I was so embarrassed by her turning off the lights, that I would use the excuse that the light bothered my mother's eyes, so she would turn off the lights. Since my mother was so strict, we decided to start saving money so that we can get married.

4

The day we told my mother about our plans to get married, she said, "You have to get engaged first. We said `` ok".

It was during the summer in September of 1971. We had gone with my family to a family members party. My boyfriend had a surprise for me that day. He surprised me with an engagement ring and we got engaged at the party. A week later we were at my house and my fiance and I tried to sneak a kiss, but we were caught by my mother and she slapped me across my face. It was so embarrassing that we never kissed again at my house.

1972

Graduated From High School

In February of 1972, four months before I graduated from high school, I transferred schools from Maxwell High School in Brooklyn to Jane Adams High School in the Bronx, so that I can be closer to home. I graduated from Jane Adams High School in June 1972. I had just turned eighteen years old in May.

Moms very strict

Me turning eighteen years old, and had graduated from High School, my mother still didn't allow me to go anywhere with or without my fiance. I recall going to the movies with my fiance one time when I graduated from high school and another time when I turned nineteen-year-old. My fiance and I went out on a double date with my older sister and her husband. This was the second time I was able to go out with my fiance after dating him for two years.

October 6, 1973

We got married

My fiance and I had saved money for two years by working all types of summer jobs to get married. On October 6, 1973, we got married. I remember the day before our wedding it was freezing cold outside. But on our wedding day, God gave us beautiful weather. It was approximately 80 to 90 degrees and sunny that day. We never had warm weather like this in New York for October in those days. We had a beautiful Church wedding and reception with lots of family and friends. This was an awesome day in our lives to remember. That day we moved to our beautiful apartment fully furnished. God has always blessed us from the very beginning.

1974

Our Son Was Born

September 15, 1974. Our son was born.

Once we were married, we decided to have our first child. I became pregnant after two months of being married. We were very happy to have had a son first because we wanted him to watch over his younger siblings.

At the time, I loved the color red and I had decorated everything red in our house. I think about it now and I am surprised that my husband let me decorate everything in the house red. It was too much. I even told my husband that the baby liked red, and to buy him a red teddy bear. My husband went out and bought a six foot tall red teddy bear for our baby. I was the one to get happy because I was the one that liked that color.

Warning signs

Several months after having my son, I went out and bought a beautiful green Dodge Charger. I wanted to buy a new car, but my instincts told me not to, because if I got into an accident, I would lose my new car. Several months later, that's exactly what happened. I was making a left turn at a light when this lady came from her right side where the cars are parked at the meters and slammed right into my auto. At that time my son was sitting in the front seat on my sister's lap. He was approximately 4 months old. In those days, there were no car seats and children can sit in the front seat of the car. The window in the passenger side where my sister sat with the baby, had broken to pieces and was all over the baby's head and everywhere. I thank God the baby or anyone else were not hurt. Unfortunately, the car was a total loss, but shortly after that, I bought a new car.

1975

Back to work

My son turned one year old, and I returned back to work. My husband and I worked Monday through Friday and always looked forward to the weekends. We loved playing paddle ball and we would play with his family members all the time.

My husband was the worst player among the men and most of the time we would lose the games, but when we played for dinner, we would get lucky and win. We always had a great time playing paddleball. Soon afterwards, we changed and started playing racquetball instead. Racquetball was better for us because the racket was lighter weight and the ball was softer. This was the only sport we ever played and loved it.

November 2008

Baby came back to life

This was on a Wednesday in November 2008. We had family members that had come to visit us at home. A group of us were engaged in conversation. My grandson was approximately 19 months at that time. He was in the middle of the living room area, and we were in the kitchen area which we can see him from where we were sitting.

My granddaughter which is his sister had been with him and she had went to the pantry to get some snacks. While she walked away, he had got a piece of waffle from the kitchen, I don't know how, but he had put it into his mouth and started to choke.

Suddenly, I looked over to him and it sounded like he wanted to cry, but he was choking and no one had realized it. Then My granddaughter heard him and went back to him. It wasn't that he was going to cry, he was choking and trying to ask for help, yet none of the adults realize it.

When his sister went back over to him, which she was six years old at the time, she carried him and tried to put him on my bed like she always did. He would usually raise his legs up to help her put him on the bed, but this time he didn't, because he was already dead and she couldn't put him on the bed, so instead, she took him and put him on the floor.

When she looked down at him, she realized he was limp. She then ran to my husband and I, and said, "Grandma, Grandpa, something's wrong with the baby."

We all ran to the room to check on the baby to see what had happened. His eyes had rolled to the back of his head and his mouth was hanging open. The baby was dead. We did not know how long he had been dead at the time. My husband grabbed the baby and carried him to the kitchen where my niece and nephew were. He then put the baby on the table, and my niece started to do C.P.R., on the baby. Then I ran to the phone to call 911. Meanwhile, the baby had been dead for approximately 15 minutes already.

Then while I was on the phone with 911, I heard my family in the background saying, "He's not coming back."

As I heard that the 911 operator told me to give the phone to someone else because I was so nervous and couldn't even think straight. I quickly gave the phone to my son and I ran to my room. As I was running across the room going to the bathroom, where my statue of Jesus was, so that I can pray, I also have a statue of the Virgin Mary, in my room and as I passed the statue of the Virgin Mary, I said something to her very quickly I don't remember what I said but I continue running to the bathroom. I was running to the bathroom to grab the statue I have of Jesus on the cross. Which I pray there very often.

When I got to the bathroom, I grabbed the statue of Jesus, kissed his hands then said, "God please, make the miracle you always make, and let the baby wake up."

I then ran back to the kitchen where they were proceeding C.P.R., and the baby immediately woke up. He came back to life. Afterwards, the police and ambulance arrived. The police took the baby in his arms, and asked that no one touches the baby. The baby was in a daze. He wasn't aware of anything that was going on. The baby went to the hospital and came out three days later. That was a miracle of God. He had no damage to his brain or anything, thank God.

A few days later, the baby must have seen himself when he was dead because he told Grandpa, I saw you and Grandma sad looking at me and crying, when I was going up to the sky. I was laughing"

Then after he said that, he started playing dead. He started rolling his eyes back, and opening his mouth like when he was dead, and was laughing. It was a very scary feeling looking at him do that. It took me back to when it had happened. We told him "Don't do that." We did not want to remember what had happened ever again. That was one of the scariest moments of our lives. I thank God that my grandson is a very intelligent boy today, and was never affected by this traumatic experience. God has blessed him with a very big miracle.

Grandpa's version

My granddaughter, the baby's sister, came to my wife and me and said "Grandma, Grandpa something is wrong with the baby." Then we all ran to the room where I picked up the baby from the floor and tried to stand him up. I then placed my hands in his stomach to do the Heimlich maneuver. The baby couldn't stand up. At that time we hadn't realized that the baby was already dead. I put him on top of the table and tried to blow the waffle down, but his body turned blue. After that my nephew's wife started to do C.P.R. on him. Five minutes later, we concluded and said, " he's dead, he's not coming back."

He had been dead for about 15 minutes by then. Nothing was working. He was cold and pale. I went to the room and I heard My wife asking God to do the miracles he always makes. I then returned to the baby and I told them, " He's dead already but I am going to blow as hard as I can into the baby.

I did it three times, but nothing happened. My nephew said," Wait, give me a minute." My nephew then blew hard into the baby's mouth. The next thing I heard was a suction- like noise and then the baby started breathing again.

This is a picture of Jesus on the cross when I kissed his hands and asked to bring my grandson back to life.

My Children and Their Families

My first born son born September 15, 1974 gave me two beautiful grandchildren. That I deeply love. He is a great son, father etc. who has a great heart and is very religious. He goes to work and always tries to get Sundays off from work so that he can attend mass with his son. He tries to spend as much time as he can with his son, he is an excellent father. He also has a beautiful 15 -year -old daughter who lives in New York and he loves very much. He tries to see her as often as he can, due to his overwhelming adoration for her. His daughter is a dancer and has won several medals. We are very proud of her.

My second born, is my daughter, she was born May 31, 1979, and she is also religious, beautiful young woman with a great heart. She gave me five awesome grandchildren. Which I deeply love. The oldest one is a girl, she's gorgeous and has a great heart. This granddaughter gave me my first great-grandbaby, which he goes to Catholic School and is very intelligent. The next oldest grandson graduated from high school and has usually worked two jobs which is very impressive. Now he is giving me another great grandbaby, which I am looking forward to seeing. Then I have two more grandsons with my second daughter that are loveable awesome kids growing up beautifully in school. My daughter is married to a wonderful very intelligent man. He is a good husband and a great father. We love him dearly.

My last born is my daughter, born August 21, 1986. She gave me five awesome grandchildren which I love deeply. She is also religious and goes to church. Her oldest daughter is now 17 years old and I am very proud of her. She graduated from High School from the 11 grade and is going to college to be a doctor. She is a very beautiful and intelligent girl. The next grandson is a handsome awesome boy which is very intelligent as well. Then she gave me three more beautiful granddaughters. She has a good husband and is happily married. They love each other very much.

I am very happy and blessed to have my three children, twelve grandchildren, and going on two great grandchildren. And also my family and friends which I love everyone very much. God bless them all.

1994 Money always appeared

In 1994, I bought my first home in Queens, New York. I was looking at the newspaper and saw these great prices for houses, so I contacted the real estate agent on the ad.

When I went to view the house I had seen in the newspaper, the realtor thought I would like other houses instead and showed me completely different houses.

At that time, I was upset with my husband and made the impulsive decision to buy a house without him. I ended up buying this beautiful house I saw.

I went home, packed up all my furniture and property loaded the truck, took our children and moved out leaving my husband behind.

Now I had to pay my mortgage and all my bills on my own. The first month before the bills were even mailed to me, I sat on my bed worried about, how I was going to pay my bills and cried. I thought to myself, "How am I going to pay these bills on my own"? I am going to lose my house and I haven't even had the house for a month yet.

I started to pray to God everyday so that I can be able to pay my bills without ever being late. I had been working for N.Y.P.D. and I started working a second job on weekends at Belmont Racetrack as security for a few months.

God has never let me down, and I was able to pay all my bills on my own, never being late on payments. Sometimes I would be a little short of money for my bills but somehow" with God's help, money always showed up for my bills. Like a miracle always happened with money. Not that I asked or received help from anyone, but it was like a miracle the money always showed up from nowhere.

Thank God. After approximately three months of being on my own, my husband and I got back together.

October 2003

In October 2003, I resigned from my job at the N.Y.P.D. as a 911 operator to make a new life in Florida for our family. I sold my house in New York and moved to Florida with my husband, children and grandchildren. After living in Florida for a few months, we weren't working at the time, so something told me to write a letter so that I can return back to work in New York. I really wasn't thinking about going back to New York at the time, but I wrote the letter anyway.

September 2004

My sister was on vacation in Buffalo, New York. When she returned home, she had gotten a message from the N.Y.P.D. (my job) for me to call them. I told her that I wasn't planning on going back to New York.

We thought we were going to have money coming in, my husband had plans to work for his sister. But when I hung up the telephone, my husband told me that he was no longer going to work for his sister and that I needed to return back to work.

I cried and eventually agreed to go back to work in New York for a while. We decided that I would return back to New York for a few months to make money, so that we can open up an ice cream store in Florida.

Then I called my job, and was told that I had missed the medical examination, and I also had another appointment for this Monday coming up. Because once you resign from your job, you have to start all the process from the beginning again.

I let them know that I was in Florida, but that I would make that appointment on Monday.

This was on Friday, when I hung up the phone, my husband and I packed up our clothing, put them into the car and the next day, which was Saturday, we were on our way to New York for my appointment to return back to work again.

Once we arrived in New York, I had one more day left to have gotten my medical examination done, otherwise I would lose my salary, vacation everything I had going on for me with seniority.

I had to think of something to do, because they weren't giving me my medical examination and I needed it to start work again with my seniority.

I couldn't afford to start as a new employee. So at that point, I made a call to a lieutenant at police plaza and told him what was going on. He said to me, "I am going to make a call and I will call you right back".

The lieutenant called me back, he made an appointment for my medical examination for the next day. Thank God. I got everything done and was back to work again, with all my seniority.

My first hug

One day, while I was at work and my family were all in Florida, I was a little sad and felt like I needed a hug. I was at a corner booth at work in N.Y.P.D., then I closed my eyes, I thought about God and I felt myself getting a hug. It was a great relief and a beautiful feeling, getting hugged by God.

Saw Virgin Mary while Sleeping

Another day while I was working in the N.Y.P.D. waiting for my time to retire, I slept over at my mom's house. I was sleeping on the right side of the bed with her, when I suddenly opened my eyes and saw the Virgin Mary near my mom's feet.

I had seen like the half body as if she were kneeling on the bed because the bed was in the way.

She was like a statue, because she didn't move. I have a statue of the Virgin Mary at home, exactly the way I saw her when I opened my eyes, so I thought that I was at home looking at my statue.

My mom has statues in her house but not this one. After I saw the Virgin Mary, I was thinking it was a statue, I closed my eyes, as I thought about it, and realized I was not at home looking at my statue, I immediately opened my eyes again, realizing what I had seen, she then had disappeared.

When I woke up in the morning, I had told my mom about seeing the Virgin Mary.

Three months later, my mother told me she also saw the Virgin Mary in the same spot that I had seen her in, but she saw her entire body in the air.

I was very excited hearing this from my mom. I had felt that we were blessed.

Afterwards, as I thought about it, I figured that the Virgin Mary didn't move when I saw her, because she knows that I am afraid at night, seeing a person move.

But by seeing her the way I did, I wasn't afraid because I thought it was my statue that I was looking at. And after seeing her, I felt happy and Blessed.

This is the picture exactly how I saw the Virgin Mary in my mother's house.

Miracle Pension

When I had started back to work again, after resigning, I heard about this pension plan that was offered to the 911 operators after I had resigned. Sadly now, before I came back to work the pension plan was no longer available.

So I drove to Nycers and I applied for the special plan they had offered while I was gone and no longer had available, hoping that I can still get it. I fill out the forms and paid back the loan in full that I had taken out with them, and was told if it goes through that I will get it.

I waited every day for an answer, and I called them all the time. I also went by the office but they hadn't heard anything yet. I was just waiting impatiently until I got an answer.

It was worth the wait. This was a miracle. It took me nine months while I waited for an answer. When I got this call at police plaza and they told me that I can retire. I asked " Can I leave now"? They said " Yes". I had to check and ask again, I said " I can leave right now"? They said "Yes"

I got up from where I was sitting and went to sign my retirement papers. This was a very happy day for me.

After I drove to sign my retirement papers, I drove back to police plaza and retired right there. I jumped up and down screaming" I'm retired" I'm retired." And said goodbye to everyone.

I received a full retirement and benefits I thank God. The next day my husband and I were driving on our way back home. I thank God for this miracle I ended up retiring.

Warnings

So many things that were happening, I soon realized that before certain things took place, I would get a fast warning. Like for an example, I will see something seconds before it happened and then it would happen, or I would think of things and then it immediately happened.

I always found it strange, but never knew why. My family and friends would always talk to me about things that were happening in there lives and I always gave them good advice, and afterwards they would tell me that I was right about the advice I had given them. I have always given good advice to everyone.

My Second Hug

After I retired, I went back to Florida. I went to Mass on Sundays as usual. While I was at the Mass, I felt as if I needed a hug again. And I did the same thing again in the church and received another hug from God. It always feels so beautiful. I felt so blessed to be able to feel this special gift and to receive all these miracles from God.

March 2009 My Daughter's Wedding Miracle

My daughter and her husband had planned their wedding day, which was March 21, 2009. Unfortunately, she needed surgery a few days before her wedding day. She had a tumor in her leg which needed to be taken out. After the doctor did the surgery and took out the tumor he damaged her nerve in her leg and gave her a drop foot. Now she had to walk with a walker. She couldn't walk at all. I was praying everyday so that on her wedding day she would be able to walk. This had to take a miracle for her to walk on her wedding day. This miracle surely happened for her, she walked down the aisle and even danced a little. She and the whole party were in disbelief. This was a great miracle for her and the rest of us. Thank God.

My Daughter's Version

Around the time of my wedding, I was using a walker to help me walk after my surgery. On the day of my wedding, I was able to walk without using my walker, it was amazing. It is a blessing to have God in my life, because he is always giving me blessings. This was a real miracle for me.

2009 Thyroid Miracle

In 2009, my grandson and I were being tested to see if we had thyroid problems.

Then, I spoke to my best friend and she had told me that thyroid medication can be taken for a period of six months and afterwards you may not have to take medication ever again.

I was so happy to have heard her say this.

I thought about it, then asked God, Please God, don't let my grandson have thyroid problems, if anything, let me take the medication for six months and never have to take it again.

Miraculously, that's just the way it happened, like I had asked God. I had to take thyroid medication for six months and afterwards never had to take it again. And my grandson came out great with no thyroid problems, thank God. I get tested every year and everything is great. Thank you God.

2011 By Miracle Got My Home

My husband and I had a friend which was visiting us. He lived across the street from us, a very sweet person. We were in conversation about the recent bankruptcy my husband and I had done back in 2009. We were conversing about the lawyer we had for the bankruptcy. He had told us that we couldn't buy another home until ten years from the date that we had filed for bankruptcy.

Our friend replied," that's not true, I can help you." We exclaimed, " You can?"

He replied," Yes." We were so happy, we were in disbelief. He use to work with the real estate agent, so he was able to help us.

Then he told us he was going to help us get the house next door that we wanted. We were so happy. So then he started to help us purchase the house next door. This was originally supposed to be our home, but the real estate agent that sold my son and daughter the first house that we were living in, had sold the house next door to this nice young couple. They had told my son and daughter that they can only qualify for one house. So now, our friend started the procedures to help us purchase this house next door.

He was half way done with this purchase, and unfortunately he passed away. R.I.P.

Now we had to find another real estate agent to finish the process that he had started. We spoke to the real estate agent that had just sold my son's house next door, we asked her if she can finish the process. She said," yes " and helped us with the final procedures to complete the house purchase. We moved into the house and had our own home again after two and a half years after filing for bankruptcy. Thank God. Then my credit was great again and I was approved for everything I applied for.

2012 Having Faith

My husband and I had driven to New York to visit my mother-in-law, which was very sick in the hospital. My husband and I were always there for her. My husband even left Florida to care for his mother in New York for several months before.

But this time, everyone had come from out of state and everywhere because they were thinking that she was going to pass away.

She wasn't eating, walking or anything, and we were all worried about her.

I went to her and having faith in Jesus, told her, "You are going to eat, walk and everything. I believe in Jesus and knew she was going to be ok. The same way I said it, miraculously it eventually happened that way. I was very happy, I knew it would happen.

Sadly approximately one and a half years later, I felt as if God was going to call for my mother- in- law soon.

So I have a sister-in-law that was very close to her mother, and was always there for her mom. I told her, "When the time comes, you have to promise me, you will take it easy because you have been the best daughter to your mom in the world. You have done everything you can for her." I was trying to prepare her for when the time came.

I was right, God had sent for her mom, it was time for my mother-in- law, to go to heaven R.I.P. She was a great mother-in-law to me, and greatly missed.

My Sons Barber

My son has a friend that cuts my son, grandson and husbands hair all the time. He is a great guy, very friendly with everyone. He had moved out of state and now is back. Before he had moved away, I would see him sometimes while he was at work, and I would say to him,"make that money." And everytime I said that to him, he would make a lot of money that day. One day he came to me and told me the story about him making money whenever I said that to him, then he told me that I was blessed.

My Plates

In July of 2013, I bought this new car and coincidentally, the department of motor vehicles sent me a plate for my vehicle and the first letter on the plate was the initial for my first name. The second letter was my initial for my last name. The third letter was B which I always said it was for "Blessed." The fourth letter was H and I always said that was for "Haven." And the last two numbers were for the year that I was born. What a coincidence that I received these plates this way.

July 22, 2014 Miracle Prayers
....

My daughter had surgery in her leg and had very bad pain. She was thinking she needed surgery again because she was having lots of problems because of her drop foot that she has. I was praying for her and I told her that she was going to be fine. The following day, she was feeling much better and was walking great again. Thank God she didn't need another surgery.

My Daughter's Version
....

I had a lot of pain in my leg and I couldn't walk. The next day, I started walking. I felt like a new person again. It was a miracle because I thought I was going to need surgery again. Thank God

August 2, 2014 A Hug from Jesus
....

It was 4:30 a.m. and I wanted to receive a hug from Jesus like in the past. I was asleep in my bed at home. I wanted to write about how it felt so that I can share it with the whole world one day. I closed my eyes and thought of Jesus. I held my arms together as if I were squeezing Jesus very tight. Then I felt myself getting hugged back. My arms were shaking. I trembled, and my heart was racing fast while I was experiencing this wonderful miracle. I thought to myself, "Maybe I shouldn't say anything because people might not believe me." People might think that I am losing it.

When I told my husband, he said that I was crazy. That was just what I expected to hear, and I said to him, "I knew it." But then he said to me." I know that you are telling the truth because you do not lie." Then I felt better by him saying that to me. He knows I don't lie, especially about something like this. And then as always I was feeling special and blessed.

January 2015 You Saved My Life

I had driven to New York with my husband to visit my mother. She had not been feeling well after my sister passed away R.I.P. on August 13, 2013.

My mother was suffering and stressed out over my sister passing away and after a while, she ended up in the hospital.

My mother was very close with my sister. They lived in the same building for over thirty years. My sister helped care for my mother, she cooked for her, put her to sleep at night, and did lots of other things for my mother.

Now my mother was losing her memory getting Alzheimer's because of losing her daughter and was not feeling well.

She ended up in the hospital. I have always prayed for my mother and family, especially at this time, I have been praying for her and asking God for special prayers for my mom every day.

As we arrived in New York, we had planned to go to the hospital to visit my mother, but by the time we got to New York, she was already out of the hospital.

When we arrived at her house, I was in conversation with her, asking her how she felt and what had happened.

She looked straight into my eyes and said to me," You saved my life." I looked at her and I was in shock. I didn't know what to say. I didn't even know what she was talking about, but I said to her," Mom I have always prayed for you. I will always say special prayers for you."

I didn't know what else to say to her because she shocked me with that statement. But today, I still wonder about that statement she said to me. What did she mean?

May 30, 2015 Angel Wings On Auto

My husband's cousin and her husband came to meet with me at my home. We had made plans to go to the flea market that day. This couple we love very much are always trying to help out with everything we need. As we all got into my husband's car, I was driving and my husband's cousin sat in the front row passenger seat near me.

As we drove down, she tells me," Look Edna! Look at those Angel Wings you have on your windshield."

I looked at my windshield and said to her, ``Oh yeah, it does look like Angel wings made out of clouds."

The Angel wings were covering the entire windshield. At that time, I wasn't realizing what had been happening with me and the Angels. If I would have thought, I would have taken a picture. But all of us in the car saw the Angel wings, and no one thought of taking a picture.

My Husbands Cousins Version

One early Saturday morning, in the spring of 2015, about 7 a.m., Edna, my husband and I were heading to Daytona Flea and Farmers Market in Daytona Beach, Florida. However, we were also saddened because my aunt Taty was extremely ill. No one knew if she would survive. Her health had been deteriorating for the past few years. My cousin Tony (Edna's husband) was in New York caring for her for several months. Edna took the wheel of the car and began driving. I was her co-pilot as we so often joked. My husband was in the back seat. The traffic was light and the weather was clear and cool, but humid. It was a beautiful Saturday morning. We were on interstate 95 driving for about 35 minutes, when I looked across the windshield and my eyes stopped in amazement. For a moment, I didn't speak. I was trying to decipher if what I was seeing was really there. I stared in astonishment and then the words came out of my mouth. Edna looked at the windshield. The image of an Angel's wing had appeared.

Edna was stunned and said, "Oh wow, I see it too."

I said to her, "This is a good sign from God that things will get better."

My husband acknowledged he also saw what we saw, the wings of an Angel. We continued looking on and talking about what it meant until it disappeared. A couple of months later, Tony returned home. Thank God Taty was better and was sent home. God is truly amazing.

May 31, 2015

The next day, after seeing the Angel wings in the windshield of the car, I glanced through my Bible, and read a little piece of the Bible. Coincidently, it was about Jesus sending Moses an Angel made from a cloud. I got the chills. I said to myself this must have something to do with the Angel on my windshield yesterday made from a cloud. I was in disbelief. I felt blessed again and was very excited. I picked up the phone and called my husband's cousin and told her what I had read and my thoughts about it. We spoke about it and were very excited about the experience.

July 2015 My Picture Wasn't Coming Out With the Angel

This was a trip I took to New York to visit my mother for her birthday on July 12, 2015.
Every year, I visit her several times a year. When I go to New York I also visit two different cemeteries where my family are buried. I always pick up my sister-in-law and go to the two cemeteries with her. This time, there was another sister-in-law that was visiting New York at her house, so she also came with us.

My husband and I picked them both up and we drove to the cemeteries and afterwards drove to the shrine.

When we got to the shrine, I walked upstairs and told my sister-in-law to take a picture of me with the Angel. When she tried to take the picture, the Angel would come out, but I wasn't appearing in the picture. So then she tried several more times to take a picture of me with the Angel. The same thing happened again. The Angel was the only one coming out in the picture.

We found it very strange, unknown why that was happening. I then went downstairs and took a picture with the Angel downstairs, and I was able to come out in that picture. I can never understand why that happened but it was very strange.

My sister-in-law Version

I went to the Shrine with my sister and Edna. We prayed and lit candles. We went to the area where the saints were located and prayed again. We took beautiful pictures with the Angels and they looked really nice. When I looked at the pictures that were taken of the Angel with Edna, Edna was always missing in the pictures. We all found it strange, but it happened over and over again. We saw an Angel without seeing Edna in the pictures. I know Edna is a very blessed person. She has seen the Virgin Mary.

September 9, 2015 An Angel In My Bathroom Seen By Grandson

My grandson was talking to me at my house, and told me that he had seen an Angel in my house in the visitor's bathroom.

I asked him," Was it a boy or a girl?"

He replied, ``A girl.'' He said that she was in her teens. He told me that he was in conversation near the restroom with his younger brother, and he looked up at her, and when she saw he had seen her, she suddenly disappeared. I was shocked and felt blessed as always. Everyone is always seeing Angels in my house and all around me.

My grandsons Version

I was in Grandma's house talking to my brother, when an Angel appeared in the bathroom. When I looked over at her, she disappeared.

December 25, 2015 Gift For Jesus

It was Christmas Day, I had just woken up, and I was thinking about all the beautiful things Jesus always does for us.

So I decided I wanted to do something special for Jesus. It couldn't be much but I was thinking of a gift for him on his birthday. I decided that Jesus wants us to be good to everyone and forgive everyone.

Since I hadn't spoken to a family member for approximately one year, I decided to give them a call to make peace with them. This was the gift that I wanted to give Jesus for his birthday, and it felt great making up with my family members. I felt very happy doing this for Jesus and myself. And I didn't expect anything back from Jesus.

Two days later, I received the best Christmas gift I have ever received. My granddaughter came knocking on my door, which I hadn't seen in three years. Her family had moved away, and I hadn't seen them at all. I couldn't believe my eyes. This was the best gift I could have ever received. Thank you Jesus.

December 2015 Angels Seen In Backyard In Clouds.

I hadn't seen my best friend from Maxwell High School in approximately 40 years. We had been trying to find each other for many years, and now we finally got in touch with each other, then we made plans to see each other in my house for December 2015. Before then, I had searched social media platforms like Classmates, Facebook etc. I was finding people with her name but never found her. She finally found me on Facebook.

After looking for each other for years, we were extremely happy to have found each other. We would call each other on the phone, and we didn't want to hang up the phone, having long conversations on the phone daily, and leading up to when we meet again. When we finally reunited, it was an awesome moment.

We were conversing in the kitchen, and I had gotten up for a moment. When I return to talk with her again, she had been looking out of my sliding doors towards my backyard and I was walking up to her. As I approached my pantry near her, she looked up and said, "Edna, look at all those Angels. You have a lot of Angels outside your house."

She saw lots of Angels in the clouds. I stood beside her near my pantry, I got the chills and said to her," Everyone is always seeing Angels all around me. I was very excited and proud to have everyone always seeing Angels all around me. I didn't know what else to say.

This is the picture where the Angels in the clouds were seen in my backyard.

January 2016 Was Told Was Going To Be A Vegetable After Surgery

My sister was going for aneurysm surgery. She had already had several surgeries in the past. The doctor had spoken to her and had advised her that she was going to be a vegetable after surgery.

I had been praying to God please make a miracle for her, and let her recover soon. Thank God he granted this miracle. The doctor also told her it was a miracle. After Surgery she did lose her memory a little but, with God's help, she is recovering slowly. My prayers are with her every day. God bless her.

April 5, 2016 Image Of Jesus on Phone

I was looking through my telephone, and suddenly, a beautiful image of Jesus on the cross appeared on my phone. However, it disappeared. I then started to look to see where it came from. I checked all my text messages but found nothing. As I continued to try to find where it had come from, it reappeared again.

Within 20 minutes, this photo of Jesus on the cross appeared two times without any clue of where it came from.

I then told my husband about what had happened, but I never saw the picture again. That was strange.

May 2017 Pain miraculously disappeared from knee

My husband and I were on our way to New York to visit my mother for mother's day.

When I woke up, I had excruciating pain in my knee, because of my arthritis. I couldn't even bend my knee or anything. I had so much pain I wanted to cry. With this happening to me, I knew that I wasn't going to be able to help my husband drive to New York.

We walked into the car and I sat in the back seat of the car with my legs straight out. That's the only way to relieve the pain.

At that time, I was feeling bad for my husband because, I couldn't help him drive. I told him, "I am sorry but I can't help you drive today. I am in excruciating pain in my knee. Then I grabbed the statue of Jesus that I have in my car, and put his hands on my knee and said, "please God let this pain go away, so that I can help Tony drive." Suddenly, after asking God to heal my pain, the pain went away immediately, like a miracle.

Then I told my husband what had happened and I went to the front of the car, and two minutes later I drove nine hours straight.

Afterwards, we drove back home, and two days later, drove back again to New York, and thank God, I had no pain for all those hours driving back and forth.

This is a statue of Jesus that I touch my knees and was healed immediately.

May 17, 2017 Image Of Jesus In The Clouds

We went to visit my mother in May for mother's day. We visited New York for approximately one and a half weeks, then returned back home to Florida.

While driving home, I was thinking about the day that my friend saw the Angels in the clouds in my backyard.

We were at the end of Georgia almost getting to Florida. So I thought to myself, let me look up to the clouds to see if I see something. As I looked up to the passenger side of the car, into the clouds, Immediately, I saw an image of Jesus right before my eyes. We Catholics know Jesus by a certain image and that's how we saw him. It was as if I were looking at a live person. He was the color of the sky. Very large image of a face that to me looks like Jesus. His hair was blowing going towards my left side. You can only see part of the shoulder, I was in shock. I couldn't hardly speak.

I looked at my husband and I said, "Tony look at that face." My husband was driving but he looked at the face and he was in shock. He didn't say a word. He looked at me, he couldn't talk, and we were both quite, none of us were able to say one word. I waited for about one minute, I didn't want to say anything because I didn't want him to think that I was losing it.

Then I asked him," Doesn't it look like Jesus?" He still couldn't talk and he nodded his head, "Yes". That was a beautiful experience we had. As we were driving away, his noise was a little off, possibly because the face was starting to disappear as we drove off.

We have been blessed to have experienced this wonderful gift. Even today it's breathtaking when I think about it.

Tony's version

While I was driving at the end of Georgia, my wife told me, "Tony look at that face," I looked up at the clouds and saw the face of Jesus. I was shocked and happy. Then my wife asked," Doesn't it look like Jesus". I nodded my head "Yes" I told my wife, "Jesus always follows you around." I kept on driving. I couldn't believe it. I was shocked. It was like Wow. His face was in the clouds like a perfect picture. When I saw the picture of Jesus in the sky, it was like his hair was blowing in the wind. It looked beautiful. The nose was a little cricket, but the rest of the face was a perfect picture. I couldn't believe my eyes.

May 18, 2017 Bible Turning Pages

This was the night after seeing the image of Jesus in the clouds. I had taken my shower before bedtime as usual. I was lying on my bed, watching my shows, suddenly my Bible which I have on top of my dresser, in my room was trying to turn pages on its own. I looked at the Bible and found the phenomenon strange.

Then I continued to watch my shows. I figured maybe it was the ceiling fan in my room that was blowing the pages from the bible, but the ceiling fan is always on and this has never happened before. Strangely the phenomenon happened again. The pages couldn't change on the Bible because I had an ankle bracelet on top of the Bible that had been broken and my husband was going to fix it. So I had left it on top of the Bible, so that my husband doesn't forgot to fix it.

I then got up from the bed and went to tell my husband. He told me that the Bible wanted me to read the page. But the Bible wasn't able to turn the pages.

This is the picture of the Bible that tried to turn pages.

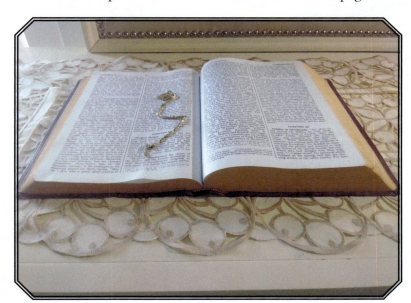

Image of Heart Appeared in Shower Curtain

That night, when I went to bed after the Bible tried turning pages, I had a gallon of Holy water under my sink that I had gotten from the shrine in New York.

When I woke up in the morning, I went to the restroom and I saw an image of a heart on my shower curtain. It was right in front of my face so that it can be seen. Then I noticed the entire gallon of Holy water had been spilled underneath my sink. The gallon wasn't broken, nor was the top of the gallon opened. It was very strange. Everything was wet under the sink. I walked over to my husband and asked him," Did you see the heart in the bathroom shower curtain. I know that was not you right?" He replied, "Maybe it was the baby."

At that time, my grandson was staying at home with us. He was about two and a half years old. And he didn't know how to write, color or anything.

So I said to my husband," You're crazy, the baby can't even color. We were both in shock, wondering what had happened.

So for the first time, since I have been getting these miracles, hours later, I thought of the idea to take a picture. I have always been in shock when a miracle happened, so I never thought of taking pictures. This time I thought of it because it was there for a while. So I took a picture and started texting it to all my family and friends. Feeling so blessed and special as always.

This is the first picture of the heart.

Now this was three weeks later, and the heart was still there. I decided," let me take another picture this will be the three weeks later picture."

After I took this picture, the picture really shocked me. The picture looked red only inside of the heart. As if it were a real heart. I couldn't believe my eyes. Again I showed it to my husband, and I started texting it to everyone again. Everybody was saying that it was the Sacred Heart of Jesus. This was so sacred to me.

This is the three week later picture that was red inside the heart.

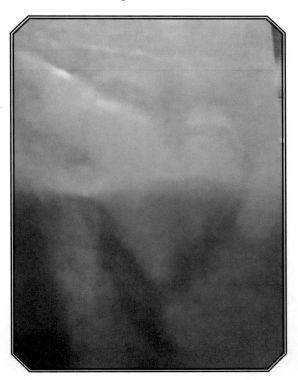

My Husband's Cousin's Version

As I recall the small red heart, I remember it had unsurprisingly appeared on a silky grey shower curtain a few days after Mother's Day. She called and told me what she had seen and sent a picture of the heart.

I was in awe over another incident happening. About a week later, I went to her home and saw it. It was breathtaking. As the months passed, the heart began fading. None of us were exactly sure what it meant. But a heart symbolizes love, the love of someone special, the love of family and friends, and the love of God. And just as it had miraculously appeared, it started to disappear.

July 2017 Share My Miracles With Priest

I had gone to New York to visit my mother for her birthday. Whenever I travel, and it's Sunday, I always try to find a church in the area and attend mass.

While in New York, I attended the Mass in Queens, that I had always attended in the past when I lived there, and after the mass, while the priest was shaking everyone's hand, as they were leaving the mass, I had briefly spoke to the priest about some of my miracles that I had experienced. I wanted to share my happiness with a priest to see what he would say. Unfortunately, he politely smiled and I was not able to speak to him at the time. He was very busy.

The next week on Sunday, I wanted to speak to another priest in Florida when I had gone back home. But it was five minutes before the mass, and he was getting ready to start the mass. I couldn't speak to him either.

I sat at the mass, a little sad, and I told my husband that I couldn't speak with the priest. Then my husband likes to joke around, so he says to me," make the lights go on and off."

After that, I really felt bad, so I got sentimental and my tears started rolling down my face. Suddenly the mass started, the priest started to give the mass and it thundered very loud. The priest looked up and said something to God, I couldn't hear what he said but then it thundered very loud again. I had never in my life heard thunder like that in church. But I told my husband," God is upset at you". My husband laughed.

August 2017 Heart Started To Fade

When the heart on my shower curtain started to fade away, I made the decision to try my best to have a priest see the heart. I took the shower curtain and made a circle around the heart so that I didn't lose the part where the heart appeared, so that I can cherish this memory forever. I then cut a circle around it and I took it to the priest before the image faded away.

August 2, 2017 Spoke to Priest

This was on a Wednesday, I didn't want the heart to fade away before I showed it to the priest. I wanted to hear what he had to say to me. I again went to the church in Florida, I walked into the rectory, although the priest was busy, he sat with me and took all the time that I needed to talk with me. I was so happy and felt so relieved to have spoken to the priest.

When I showed the priest the heart, he could still make out the shape of the heart,

It was still very visible. He told me that he believed me. He said that God loves me and that miracles happen all the time. He had also said other things to me about God, but I was so excited to have spoken to him that I didn't remember what he had said. I was so happy to finally get this off my chest.

After I spoke to this priest, that's when I made my decision to write a book. I had been writing my experiences as they happened over the years, but never thought that I will be writing a book about my miracles. I had written down what had happened and the date, but now I am going to share my happiness with the world.

The Heart

I cut around the heart shape to cherish it forever. This way I know exactly where the heart shape is. When I was cutting around it, it felt as if it were real. This heart is very sacred to me.

This is the original heart now.

August 30, 2017 Sister's Headache Disappeared

I called my sister on the phone, and we were in conversation, afterwards we started talking about the miracles that I had experienced and that were occurring in my life. There are lots of miracles that I have experienced, so we were on the phone for a while.

While in conversation, she then started telling me about her excruciating pain she had in her head. She had so bad of a pain, she wanted to hang up the phone. She said she wanted to take a warm shower to see if that would alleviate the pain.

She was telling me, "This is the worst pain that I have ever had, I have gotten headaches all my life but never like this."

She told me how scared she was from the pain she had. I felt so sorry for my sister, I felt her pain. Then, I looked up at the picture of Jesus that I have on my mirror in my room. Suddenly, Jesus must have seen the pain that I felt for my sister. He knew I wanted her to feel better, then I started telling her, "I am going to pray for you to feel better."

I said to her," God Bless You. You are going to take a shower then you are going to bed and when you wake up, you are going to feel much better."

As I was telling her that statement, she interrupted the conversation and said," Hold up, Hold up, it's going away. My headache is going away." I feel like a new person!

She told me that she got the chills and that the experience was like a miracle. I was so happy she was feeling much better and also experienced a miracle God send her while talking to me.

My Sister's Version

I was sitting there with a pain in the right side of my head. It felt as if my head was going to explode.

As I am talking to Edna, I interrupted the conversation and told her," The pain is slowly ceasing."

Suddenly, something like a breeze came to my head and the pain went away like a miracle. I felt like a new person.

August 31, 2017

The following day, my sister called me and said to me, "Please do whatever you did yesterday, because I have pain today."

I said to her that, I didn't do anything. All I did was say I was going to pray for her, but God felt my pain also, and he is the one that immediately made her feel better. I felt as if Jesus felt my sorrow that I was feeling for my sister, while I was staring at his picture, and he immediately made her feel better.

I told her, "I will pray for you today, so that you can feel better again. I was very happy to have had another miracle for my sister and a witness for another miracle that God has made. I told God," Thank you, God."

November 28, 2017 Light In My Backyard

It was my granddaughter's birthday party. She was turning 16 years old. Her father wanted to throw her a big party in a club, but she refused. Then I asked her if she wanted me to make the party in my house. She also refused.

Three months before the party, she decided that I can make the party for her in my house. I started making plans and inviting everyone. Her birthday was almost here, and I started to get knee pains again a few days before the party. I was worried about having to stand all day, cook and clean. I also wanted to dance for the party.

I started praying to Jesus, so that the pain can go away. Right before the party, the pain had gone away. I was able to do everything I had to do plus, I danced all night and had a great time. And my knee pain went away for possibly more than a year. I was afraid of the pain returning the next day from all the dancing I had done, but the pain didn't return, Thank God.

And while we partied, in the backyard, I didn't have much light in the backyard, and all of a sudden, when it got dark, my granddaughter's grandma, said to me, "Wow look at that moon. It's bringing us lots of light." We had a full moon in my backyard. I said to her," God is sending us light.

March 25, 2018 Jesus Sending Message

This was Palm Sunday. My husband and I were in New York. We had went to Mass in Queens where I had gone for years when I lived in New York.

As I walked inside the Church, everyone in the earlier Mass were coming out of Mass. And other people were going into Mass. So the priest was shaking everyone's hand, and as I went to shake his hand, he looked at me, and said to me," I love you."

I said to him, I love you too." He looked at me and said," I know you."

But I looked at him strange, because I didn't know him. I had never seen him in my life. Then he hugged me. I felt very special and blessed. I felt so special that I trembled. I was picked out of a crowd and was told that I was loved and I had gotten a hug from the priest.

At that time, I had been worried about my mom. She was not feeling very well. This made me feel as if Jesus was sending me a message saying that he loved me, and everything was going to be okay. I spoke to the priest for a few minutes and told him that I had written a book about miracles.

After I got back home, I called him and told him that, I felt that I was getting a hug from Jesus. And also felt as if Jesus was talking to me through him. I also told him about some of my miracles that I have had. He was very happy. I also send him my book about miracles so that he can read it. Now Every time I see him when I go to Mass, he's my best friend.

March 28, 2018 Strangely Speaking

We had been visiting in New York. The family decided to have a family gathering in my mother's house. My mom wasn't feeling very well.

My mother was talking, but we couldn't understand what she was saying. She had been getting worse with Alzheimer's disease. But we were all happy to be there with her.

I had been a little upset with my sister, because of a misunderstanding we had before. But that day, we were all happy to be together.

When I was getting ready to leave, I walked upstairs to my sister's house, hugged her and told her that I loved her.

As she was walking away, I felt as if Jesus was telling me what to say to her. I told her, " I really love you. I mean it, give me another hug, I am sorry."

It was very strange, the way the words were coming out of my mouth. Great words were coming out of my mouth without me realizing it, as if Jesus was speaking through me.

It reminded me of the time when the priest in the church, had spoken to me and said that he loved me and hugged me.

At the time, I had felt as if it were Jesus hugging me and trying to tell me, everything was going to be ok with my mom and brother.

So now, I felt great telling my sister what I said to her. She also said it back to me then walked away.

April 24, 2018 No More Muscle Spasms

When I woke up in the morning, I was feeling so happy and thankful to Jesus, because when I use to wake up every morning and stretch my legs, in the past, I would get muscle spasms. My muscles in my legs would pop out and I use to get excruciating pain. My husband always had to run to me and message my muscles in my leg, so it can go back into place.

But today, I woke up and forgot, so I stretched my legs and had no pain, the muscle didn't pop out. Every morning, I try not to forget and stretch my legs, but if I do stretch I stop myself because I get scared that the muscle spasms will come back.

Before, as soon as I attempted to stretch, my muscles will pop right out. Ever since I had prayed to Jesus on my granddaughter's birthday to heal me, I haven't got any pain in my knees. And until today's date, I haven't woken up with muscle spasms on my legs. Thank God. When I opened my eyes, I thought about it and said,"WOW, thank you Jesus."

Having faith my brother will heal from cancer

My brother lives in Queens, and has found out he had cancer since March 27, 1018. He was told by the doctor that they couldn't do anything for him. The cancer was spreading. He had stage 4 cancer.

I was very worried for him, but I know God is more powerful than anything in the world. I started praying for him everyday, asking God to make a miracle for my brother.

My brother has changed his life around lately. He attends Mass on Sundays, helps out in church, and he has said all his life, he has had lots of miracles happen to him. He and I believe God is going to make another miracle for him and give him a second chance in life.

June 28, 2018 God cleared the way

The alarm rang at 4 am, I woke up ready to go back home to Florida, we had been in New York. There were bad thunderstorms in effect for mostly all of our trip going back home, it was kind of scary, but I wanted to go back home already. We had been in New York long enough.

When I woke up a 4 am, there had been loud thunderstorms going on, I was hearing the storms for several hours already, so we decided to stay for another day and we went back to sleep.

After going back to sleep, I woke up at 8 am and decided, we were leaving and made a fast breakfast, some French toast so we can hurry up and leave to Florida because at that time there were no storms passing by.

My husband, grandson and I got ready and started on our way back home by 10:28 am, this is the latest time we have ever left for a long ride like this, but we all got enough rest before we left, and when we get home we have our parking, so that's no problem, looking for parking.

Now we were wishing we have good weather going home. On our way home, God gave us a sunny day and we were expecting terrible weather, thank God.

We had some traffic on the Cross Bronx Expressway and Virginia because of leaving so late. But other then that our ride was great so far.

Then we got to North Carolina, and I was in the back seat feeding my grandson some pizza we had just picked up to eat.

All of a sudden, I hear my husband saying something. I looked up and saw it was starting to rain hard, the clouds were very dark and there was lighting it looked scary. I was thinking, oh no, this storm is going to start now, we are going to get caught in it, oh no, please don't let this storm come down on us, and said a little prayer, all of a sudden there was no rain and it got sunny on our ride all the way home Thank God. This was a great blessing.

July 7, 2018 Tony's pain in ear.

My husband was up all night long with a very excruciating ear ache. He couldn't sleep all night in pain.

While I was sleeping all of a sudden I opened my eyes, he was twisting and turning in pain and told me about it and I felt so bad for him, he complained about pain all night. He told me he has to go to the doctor in the morning.

I said a prayer for him and asked Jesus to please let his pain go away. When we woke up in the morning, I asked him, are you going to the doctor? How's your ear? He replied " I have no pain. The pain went away. I smiled and said Thank God, I prayed for your pain to go away. He told me thank you, your prayers always help, it did go away.

August 12, 2018 Jesus Picture Appeared On Phone

It was on a Sunday morning. My husband and I had attended the 10 a.m. mass, we mostly go to the later mass but, my son got a new job and now had to work on Sundays.

My son attends the mass services on Sundays before work every week. My grandson likes to go to mass with his father, he goes to a different church and there are activities for him while at services with his dad. So he enjoys going with his dad. Therefore we went to the early mass in the Catholic Church where we go. Then when my son finished the services at the church where he attends, he bought my grandson to us after our mass so that my son can resume to work.

While my husband and I were at mass, I always pray for my entire family, that day I prayed especially for my mom and my brother. I had asked Jesus to please help my brother, he is fighting cancer, and he was told a few months before, that they can't do surgery on him, and that the cancer was spreading. I have been praying to God since I heard about my brother's condition, so that God can help him. At that time, I was also worried about my mother that had been put in the nursing home.

While I was at the mass, I looked at the image of Jesus on the cross in church and said," Please help my family, especially my mother and brother. I prayed with so much faith. When I left the mass, and I was going into my car, something told me to look through my pictures in my phone.

As I was glancing through my pictures, this unbelievably beautiful, colorful, blinking picture, caught my eye. One of the colors that I first spotted was bright orange. Then the blinking of the heart in the picture. It was so beautiful that I had to look at this picture. It blinked on and off like a heartbeat. The thing about it was that the picture was with my saved pictures as if I had saved it. When I touched the screen on my phone to look at it, it was the picture of Jesus on the cross, I had never seen this picture in my life before. It had a white heart around Jesus on the cross. It had appeared right in between my mother's picture and my brother's picture. Like if Jesus was answering my prayers.

Then we got into the car and while my husband was driving, I said to him," Look at this beautiful picture that appeared between my mother's and my brothers picture." He said to me," Someone must have sent it to you." I said," No," it's with my saved pictures as if I had saved it in my phone. But I never saw this picture before.

He couldn't understand what I was trying to tell him, because he doesn't know much about phones and saved pictures. I said to him," You are the only one here and I want you to see it and try to understand what I am talking about. Then he finally understood what I was trying to say to him. I said to him," You always have to try to understand when I say something important to you, because you are the one that's always with me, and I want to share all my special experiences with you. He said to me, 'Yes, I understand."

I then started texting and sharing my miracle to everyone. I felt so excited and blessed that my tears rolled down my face. Everyone loved this picture, and had something beautiful to say about it. My sister-in-law told me she will say special prayers with this picture.

What a coincidence, I had went to pick up something at McDonalds for my grandson, after mass that day and the bill came up to $7.77. I heard these are the numbers for haven. We are always blessed. Thank you God.

This is the picture that appeared between my mother's picture and my brother's picture after the mass.

September 11, 2018 God Always Hears Prayers

It was 9:43 p.m. I was asleep, I had been very tired, so I went to bed early that day. My daughter calls me up and I didn't answer the phone because I was asleep.

She then calls me again, and I woke up and answered the phone. She tells me that she had been in the hospital for two days. I asked her, "Why didn't you call me?" She replied," I didn't want to worry you! I asked her?" What happened?" She replied, my white blood cell count was too high, so they left me in the hospital, and now it's even higher. So she's explaining to me that one of the patients in the hospital just passed away from an infection they had, and she was so scared. So she called me so that I can pray for her. I replied," Of Course." I was worried for her, I immediately said a prayer for her. I told her she will be much better for her next blood count, and that she was going home the next day.

When we finished the conversation, I got up from my bed and send her a text with a special blessing saying to feel better. The next thing I did was, I got on my knees and prayed to Jesus to bless her and let her feel better so she can go home.

The next day, I was trying to get in contact with her and she never answered the phone. I wanted to go visit her in the hospital, but I didn't know if she was still in the hospital. She lives four hours from me, so I had to wait to hear from her. I didn't know if anyone was home, so I couldn't even go to her house. If I would have went there, and no one was home, I wouldn't have known where to go. I tried calling all her family, still no answer.

The following day I had called again and finally got through. She told me that she came home the day after I spoke to her. She said to me, "Thank you for praying, the prayers really worked, Thank God."

October 9, 2018 Cleared Passage

We had intentions on driving to New York in the morning. But there was a hurricane warning in effect. My husband woke up at 5 a.m. and said to me," we should leave to New York now. I asked him," You want to go now? I thought the storm was going to start in the morning, so we planned to leave at night." He said, "Yes." I asked, "You sure?" He said, "Yes." I said, "Let's go."

We had made plans to leave at night time, but we were trying to beat the hurricane so we got ready and were on our way to New York.

While we were driving, it attempted to rain a few times. There was like a rain shower in our windshield. At one point it started to rain very hard that you couldn't see out. I got scared and I thought we were going to take several days to get to New York if the rain didn't stop. I asked God," Please God, Clear the passage for us the way you did in your days, that you cleared the passage for your people to pass through the water.

Soon after I said that, we had sun and good weather, all through our entire trip Thank God. He surely cleared the passage for us.

We were making this trip, for my first book signing. Unfortunately, almost every time we make plans to go to New York, we usually go on the wrong days with bad weather conditions, but God always gives us a safe trip and good weather.

As we were on our way to New York, there was a tractor trailer that had crashed into the divider and went into the grass on 95S, and also a car accident on 95N. But thank God, we had great weather and got there safe.

Now we were in New York, my husband got sick with a bad cold. We were going to see my mother every day and I was afraid that he would get my mom sick.

The following week, my sister was scheduled to get another aneurysm surgery and we wanted to be there for her, but we had to leave so that she wouldn't get sick either. I felt awful, I couldn't be there for her. But we didn't want them getting sick. Now my husband was sick and he had to drive home. He likes to do all the driving, he doesn't want me driving, so we tried to go home before he felt any worse.

An Angel
....

On our way home that day, my husband felt fine, thank God. We had got to the end of South Carolina, I was looking out of the window while my husband was driving, all of a sudden, I am staring at the front windshield window, and I see, a very big cloud that looked like an Angel's face and the face was looking to the left. And it looked like the Angel could have been a girl, you can see part of the shoulder and the Angel wings were very large. It was late so it had been very dark outside.

My husband asked me? "What are you looking at?" I replied," Doesn't that look like an Angel? And I pointed to the Angel. My husband said, "Yes."

It was very dark out, I attempted to take a picture but the picture wasn't coming out. The picture came out very dark, like a black sky and a small light. So I couldn't get a picture of the Angels face. It was a beautiful experience as always.

October 27, 2018 Miracles Always Happening

I woke up this Saturday morning and felt one of my bones on my right foot was strange.

The next day it hurt a little. It was Sunday, we had gone to Mass, before the mass, we told my grandson, we would take him to the park if he behaved in mass.

He did behave, so we took him to the park after mass. I told him we will do whatever he wants to do in the park, so he chose to ride his bike in the jogging tracks, so I walked the track while he rode his bike.

After the walk my foot started to hurt when we arrived home. The next day, my foot was swollen from where that bone was and from me walking in the park.

My husband asked me if I wanted to go to the doctor. I replied, ``No.'' I don't like going to doctors, unless I really need to go.

Afterwards, I decided I would go to the doctor because I really couldn't walk. So we went to the doctor and I was sent for blood tests and x rays.

The following day, I still couldn't walk so I figured I would take both test for the same day, which was 10–31–18.

Now I was on my way to my appointment, but I had excruciating pain that I needed a walker to walk. I couldn't even walk with the walker because my right foot was swollen with pain, and I had problems with my right arm for approximately 2 years. So I couldn't use my right arm.

Now I have been putting my weight on my left leg and I was afraid of hurting my left leg by putting all the pressure and weight on it.

When I was called in for the blood test, they had to help me, I almost fell.

Then we had finished at the blood test, and had to go for x rays. As we got to the next appointment, there was no parking in the front of the medical center. So my husband parked the car across the street. We were not thinking at the moment and forgetting that I couldn't walk, I started to cross the street and was struggling across the street.

I had to take breaks between every 4 steps it was horrible. I was tired, my left leg and right arm were taking a beating.

My husband ran into the medical center to see if they had a wheelchair for me.

As I was struggling to walk while my husband got back with the wheelchair, this wonderful lady asked me," Can I help you?" I sadly replied," No thank you, there's nothing you can do. Thank you." She said to me," God bless you." and walked away.

As I kept struggling, I almost tripped over my slippers, and I then hurt my foot even worse.

Now I am crying. Another wonderful lady comes to me and asked," Can I help you?" I replied," No thank you, my husband just went to see if they have a wheelchair inside. I just hurt my foot." I was crying because I have pain. She said," I know how you feel, I broke my foot before. I am going to see about the wheelchair." And she walked away, and came back and said," He's coming out with the wheelchair. She stood with me while my husband came out. God bless her, she was awesome.

Then my husband came out with the wheelchair, and it was such a relief to sit down.

After almost falling again, my foot got even more swollen like a football. Afterwards, I went home, and I was in bed I couldn't walk at all.

My husband had to do everything for me. He was awesome, he is always great to me when I don't feel well. God bless him.

Then I told my husband," I should be walking by Saturday" This was Thursday, I was worse at that time, then when it first happened, because of almost falling.

I prayed to God asking God to heal me. I wanted to get on my knees, to pray for special miracles for myself, but I couldn't move my foot, it was swollen and numb. I was afraid of falling and hurting myself even more.

On Friday morning, I felt safe enough to get on my knees to pray for my special miracles, and I got on my knees and put the statue of Jesus hands on my foot and asked him to help me feel better and let me walk.

I was in bed the entire day. My swollenness was almost all gone.

At approximately 11:53 p.m. I told my husband, "I am going to try to walk." I got up and walked to the restroom very slowly. My husband and I were so excited. It felt as when a new baby was trying to walk. My husband said to me joking," come to daddy" as if he were talking to a baby that was learning how to walk.

The next day, Saturday, I woke up and started to walk the way I had told my husband that I would. It was a miracle for the way I was feeling to heal so quickly after my prayers. Thank God

November 2018 Miracles Always Happening

My husband had gone to the doctor, he had been diagnosed with high pressure in the past and high cholesterol. But today he was told that they were both high, that he was diabetic, and had C.O.P.D., and also that he had lungs of a 107 year old man.

He was given diabetic medication and also was told to check his blood every day for two weeks.

When he tried to get the medication prescribed to him, his coverage didn't approve it, because he had to have the Blood glucose monitoring system first to test his blood.

Therefore he didn't take the diabetic medication. But he took the blood test for diabetes that was requested by the doctor for two weeks.

Since the age of 14 years old, my husband had been smoking. Now I was worried about him, he wouldn't stop smoking. He had tried to stop smoking in the past several times but could never stop.

I was wondering, how long are his lungs going to last? All I did was cry, worried about how long in life does my husband have left. I didn't want to lose my husband.

When I woke up in the morning, I went to him crying, and told him that" I don't want him to die". I need him in my life. Please stop smoking.

He then realized how I felt and realized he was hurting himself. With my prayers every day, and after this serious talk I had with him, he listened to me, and stopped smoking overnight. It was like a miracle. He had tried to stop smoking many times before, but he never succeeded.

So now he started doing exercise, and eating the right foods to lose weight.

Then he was due back to the doctor for results. He went to the doctor and while we were in the doctor's office waiting for the doctor to come in the room, she knocks on the door and comes in the room with a happy face.

She had a big smile on her face. She said to him," I haven't seen this before. You did great. Your numbers are low. We all had big smiles on our faces. She just advised him to keep checking his blood level.

Now my husband has been doing great. No C.O.P.D. or diabetes, Thank God. That's the reason why his medication wasn't approved. There's always a reason for things that happen in life. Thank God, this was a miracle.

December 20, 2018 More And More Miracles

My sister had an aneurysm surgery in the past, and she was advised that she was going to be a vegetable. But with God's help she came out great.

Now December 20, she was going for surgery again, in her head as before but this time she had a bump and blood on the aneurysm.

I was so worried about her. I prayed for her every day. When she went in for surgery, I waited for her husband to call me at home. I wasn't able to go to New York for her surgery. I had just came back from New York. All of a sudden my phone rings while I waited for the call. I saw the first letter of the name in my phone which started with A so I thought it was my son.

I answered the phone, what's up. My sister said,"Hello." I said," Elizabeth," it was my sister. I was so happy to hear her voice, her voice was clear and she sounded great. I couldn't believe it was her. She had just had surgery, and she was doing great. I thank God for all he always does for all.

March 3, 2019 Image of Jesus appeared on phone

This was on a Sunday. My grandson, husband and I were getting ready to go to Mass, when my son calls my house to speak to his son that he had stayed over our house for the weekend.

My grandson has had lots of miracles, God has blessed him. As he was speaking to his father, out of nowhere, he comes out and says "Jesus Christ."

As he said those words an image of Jesus appeared on my cell phone. I showed it to my husband and my son heard me talking about it over the phone. My sons friend was with him and questioned him. He told her it was an image that appeared on my phone.

It was very surprising the way that happened but I tried to find the image and it disappeared, I never saw the image again. I questioned my grandson and asked him who had talked to him about Jesus Christ because he always says Jesus. He said " I said it myself." I said to my husband "wow".

March 16, 2019 Pain Goes Away

This was on a Saturday, my husband and I had started to work on a design pavement in front of the house.

We had worked on it for hours. From approximately 9 a.m. until about 6 p.m.

This was the hardest work I have ever done in my life. I was helping my husband with the pavements, but I had no plans on mixing cement, because it looked like hard work mixing cement, and that's not the type of work that I do.

As we were working, my husband was working very hard, doing lots of things at once. I felt sorry for him, while he worked on one thing, I tried to mix an 80 lb. bag of cement to help him out.

As he finished what he was working on, he didn't let me finish mixing the cement that I had started. He finished it instead.

I then continued to help out with the pavements.

By the time we had finished the pavements, it was a long day. I was so exhausted, I went into the house to take a shower.

While in the shower, I couldn't even stand up of how tired my legs felt. I was struggling in the bathtub trying to stand up, to take a shower.

After my shower, I layed on my bed and asked my husband to please bring me a glass of water, I felt very dehydrated.

I never like to drink anything while I am doing any type of work, I do this all the time.

As I was lying on my bed, my legs felt as if I had 500 lbs. of cement on each leg. I couldn't move my legs at all.

Before I fell asleep, I prayed to Jesus to help me feel better, I needed prayer so bad. The next day, I woke up and felt better, I was able to get up and slowly walk to the restroom. This was on a Sunday, but I still wasn't walking very well. I told my husband," I am not going to be able to go to mass."

For me to miss mass, I really have to be feeling sick. I said to him," I still can't walk very well." Then I said, " I am going to lay back down to see if I feel better so that I can go to mass.

I laid back down and 30 minutes later, my legs felt like a new person. I was able to walk like nothing had ever happened.

I went to mass right after that and I was even able to kneel down through the entire mass without any problems. Every time this happens to my knees, I can't kneel down or anything of how bad my knees get and I was able to kneel down through the entire Mass. Thank you Jesus.

March 22, 2019 My brothers miracle

Last year in March 27, 2018, my brother was told that he had stage 4 cancer and there was nothing that can be done for him. He was also told by the doctor that the cancer was spreading on his body. I was so scared because we had two persons in my husbands family last year that were told they had stage 4 cancer and passed away within 2 months. But there is nothing impossible for our God.

News we waited for happened miraculously.

This is the best news I've heard since last year in March from my brother. My brother just text me and told me he just came back from the doctor. After all the radiation he has been through, medication etc. today he went to the doctor and he was told they can't find any cancer in his body. But he was told that he still has to take medication for the rest of his life. My tears came out of how happy I was. Only Jesus makes these miracles happen all the time. I can never stop thanking Jesus for everything he has done for us always. All you have to do is believe in Jesus, have faith, pray and you get miracles all the time. I have been sharing this great news with the world today of how happy I am.

March 23, 2019 After finding out my brothers miracle

It is 11:35 am. I just finished speaking to my brother today after finding out yesterday when he had texted me to let me know that the Doctor didn't find any cancer in him. I didn't have much time to speak to him yesterday because when he had texted me the great news, he said he was going to sleep so that he can be awake when his girlfriend comes home from work.

I have been so happy that I started telling everyone the great news and I also put it on Facebook and everywhere. My brother told me that the Doctor told him the only way this could have happened is by a miracle.

Last year in March, when my brother went to the doctor, that he had found out he had cancer, before he had his procedures, I had spoken to the doctor and told him his hands were blessed and he was going to make a miracle for my brother, and the doctor looked at me and smiled.

With God's help the doctor made that miracle happen one year later. My brother said he has had so many miracles that people have come to him so that he can write a book, but he told me, he's too busy for that. He thanked me for praying for him. I told him " I would never stop praying for you". I will continue praying so that the cancer doesn't come back. God has always blessed him. Thank you God. Right now I am the happiest person on earth.

March 30, 2019 A heart appeared out of shower mist

I went into my room then entered my bathroom to take a shower.

When I came out of the shower, I was putting on my lotion and I looked at the mirror and I saw a heart, made of the shower mist on the bathroom mirror. I was shocked seeing another heart in my bathroom.

I tried to take a picture of the heart in the mirror, but it didn't come out.

When you open the door the heart disappears, because it was made out of fog. And everytime you take a shower, you can see the heart was still there.

I showed my husband the heart in the mirror and he said that he had cleaned the mirror in circular shapes. I said to him, "Look at the heart" it's a heart shape, then he said "Yes your right.

Then I thought about the two more hearts that had appeared on another shower curtain in the same spot, that the first heart had appeared on in the past.

These two hearts appeared about a month ago, they were on the curtain as if they were ironed on the shower curtain. I took a picture of these two.

Meanwhile the heart in the mirror stood there until my husband cleaned the bathroom than cleaned the mirror. That was strange the way the hearts keep appearing all the time. It's a blessing.

April 19, 2019 Expecting a rain storm

This was Good Friday. I was going to the Mass of the Stations of the Cross which I try to go every year. The Mass was at 3 pm. We were expecting a rain storm for that time. By 2 pm I was already dressed up for the Mass. I had my grandson and my husband with me in the house ready to go to mass, but they weren't dressed yet.

At 2 pm, it started raining hard with thunderstorms. I am afraid of thunderstorms because I have got caught in one before and had a terrible experience. I had made a wrong turn on my way home because I couldn't see where I was driving, the rain was coming down very strong. When I was driving home, I thought I was going to drive into a dish, all I did was cry, I was so scared of getting into an accident, so now I don't like driving in a storm.

It was 2 pm and the bad weather had started. Then my brother called me and told me he was going for surgery. This was about the third surgery in the same hip he has got done. We were talking about the surgery and I told him I wasn't going to church because of the weather.

Then I said to him, the rain just stopped, I had changed my clothes but I am going to change again to go to the Mass. I am going to make this Mass special for you.

I hung up the phone and changed my clothes again into church clothes. I asked God, please don't let me have bad weather, at least let me get to church and come back home and don't let it thunderstorm while I am driving. I left to church and I had good weather, came out of the church and it was still good weather so I said, I am going to the supermarket to go shopping because the weather is good.

I went in the supermarket took my time and shopped and as I finished paying for my grocery it started raining like crazy. I walked out and got soaked and wet. I had to go back into the supermarket and wait until it stopped raining a little. Then I drove home. It rained hard but no thunderstorms thank God. If I would have came straight home, I would not have gotten any rain, but I took it for granted and went shopping. But I had a safe trip home, thank God. God is with me all the time.

April 21, 2019 Tombstone Picture appeared on my phone

This was Easter Sunday. I went to Mass with my husband and after mass I happen to look at my phone and saw this beautiful picture of when Jesus rose on the 3rd day from his death from his tombstone. This picture had appeared on my phone in my saved pictures as if I had saved this picture with pictures I had taken in the past. This happens every time a special picture appears on my phone. I always get these beautiful pictures of Jesus appearing on my phone for special things that are happening in my life. It's a beautiful feeling.

May 3, 2019 Miracle With knife

This was on a Friday. After I went to visit my mom which I visited her everyday while being in New York.

We drove back to my brother- in- law's house in New York, which we stay in his house every time we go to New York.

While at his house, I had to take my cholesterol medication which now I started to take half a pill instead of a whole pill so I had to cut the pill in half.

My brother–in–law has this old knife that belonged to his mom in the past in his house. The way it's shaped it looks like the opposite side of it is the side you use to cut. I got confused and was using the wrong side of the knife.

As I was trying to cut my cholesterol medication in half with the knife, I was forcing the knife against my thumb, the knife was upside down instead of towards the pill, and I didn't even realize it, until the pill wasn't cutting up.

Afterwards I realized what I was doing. I had the knife upside down trying to cut with the wrong side of the knife, I thought I had cut my finger, so I stopped and ran to the bathroom and told my husband what I had done.

He was giving me alcohol to put in my hand which I thought I had cut up. I said, `No that's going to burn, give me peroxide."

So he then spilled peroxide on my hand, near my thumb. I was thinking I almost cut my finger off. I had a mark on my finger but no blood.

When I looked at my finger after putting peroxide on it, I had no marks or anything on my finger. I was in shock that was a miracle because it was for my finger to be severe. I went back to cut up my cholesterol pill and it cut up right away with the same knife, after using the correct side of the knife to cut it.

Thank God he is always watching over me. The next time I went to my brother- in- law's house, I forgot about that knife again, and I was starting to use it the wrong way again, and he took the knife and hid it or throw it away, I am not sure what he did with that knife. But he disappeared it, so that I wouldn't use it again.

Please, be careful with knives. This is just a miracle that happened to me, and God helped me.

Shoulder Healing

Every morning, after my shower, and at night time, I always pray to God to bless my entire family, friends and the world.

I always have so many family members that I pray for every day, and friends that need prayers.

At one time I wondered, am I asking God for too much, because it's so many people that need my prayers every day that I pray for. But I know it's never too much for God. He is always there for everyone, and he is always answering prayers.

He has been healing me all my life. I had been in excruciating pain in my shoulder, that I couldn't even move my arm for approximately two and a half years all together.

I had went to the doctor and he looked at me like feeling sorry for me, thinking it was arthritis and nothing was done. I couldn't raise my arm without the help of the other hand. I could hardly move my arm.

Then I went to another doctor, he said that I possibly have a torn ligament and might need surgery, because if it were arthritis, I would be able to move my arm. I went home and started to think, I am not getting surgery. I am going to pray to God that my shoulder gets better.

Then little by little, my shoulder started to get better and it took a little while, but now I am back to normal without surgery. My cousin's husband had the same problem, and he had to get surgery, I Thank God that I didn't need the surgery.

May 5, 2019 No damage to auto

We had just returned home from New York, that day we were emptying out the auto that we drove to New York, and I was putting things away that we had bought back home with us from New York, into the garage.

When I opened the garage door and looked at my auto that I had in the garage, I was very upset. I have an outdoor pool stored in my garage that each part weighs approximately 100 lbs. I had this pool in the garage on the shelf and the parts fell and hit my auto.

The parts were leaning against the auto when I went into the garage. I keep this auto in the garage so that it can be safe and I come home and all these parts and some other things that were in the garage had come down and fell on my auto, I was so upset.

I called my neighbor and asked her if something had happened in the area while I was away. She tells me we had some winds but she doesn't see how all those things can have fell down.

After I saw this I didn't even want to look at my car to see the damage in my car. I went to bed and the next day, I drove my car out of the garage and looked to see if there was any damage to the auto.

But boy was I surprised, there was no damage to the auto. I thank Jesus that was a miracle.

May 11, 2019 Reminds me of the image of Jesus we saw in the clouds

This was on a Saturday the day before Mother's day. This friend of mine that's also on Facebook, had put up a picture in Facebook for mother's day of hers, and on the right side of the picture it had a little writing which said to click on it to try it, so I did.

There were lots of background pictures to choose from but I thought of scrolling down to the pictures on the bottom, and so I did.

As I scrolled down, I spotted this picture which caught my eye. Then I clicked on it and my picture went into it with this beautiful background, so I liked what it looked like and I put it as my profile picture in Facebook.

When I really looked at it, I realized that this picture reminds me of the image that my husband and I saw in May 2017 of Jesus in the clouds.

But the image of Jesus that we saw was on the passenger's side of the car in the clouds, which was on my side of the auto while we were driving on the road.

This picture of mine, which is on this page is almost the same way we saw the image, but the only difference is that my picture is in the front of the road.

The image of Jesus was so beautiful breathtaking, large and clear; this picture reminds me so much of that day. I can never forget it. I showed it to my husband and he said WOW. It reminds him of that image also.

I love this picture because of that and I will save it forever.

This is a picture of me, reminds me of the image we saw of Jesus in the clouds.

May 29, 2019 Jesus always hears prayers

This was on a Wednesday. I was feeling lots of tightness in my chest, pain in my head, sharp needle pain in the left side of my neck and felt disoriented. I was very scared, I felt as if I had gotten a minor stroke. I wanted to go to the hospital but I didn't go because I had my sister-in-law coming over on May 31 for my daughter's birthday and I had lots of things going on for this weekend. If I would have gone to the hospital they would have left me in the hospital. So that keeps me from going, I didn't want to stay in the hospital. So I thought of calling my doctor to let her know what had happened to me, but then I decided if I call her she is going to send me to the hospital and I had no plans on going to the hospital, so I didn't call her because then she will be upset with me.

I figured I will see my doctor in a few weeks that I had an appointment. I prayed to God so that I can feel better, I thank God I felt better the next day I just felt disoriented. On the third day It was like everything just went away and nothing had happened. I never went to the hospital. Thank God everything went well.

June 1, 2019 Lifted up to safety

My daughter was going to the hotel that my granddaughter had rented for her and her family for her birthday. So she had invited my husband and I to go spend the day at the pool with the family, so that I can get my mind off worrying about my brother that just passed away R.I.P. yesterday.

I wasn't going to go but I decided to go to get this off my mind I didn't want to believe what had just happened to my brother. So we went to meet them at the hotel.

When we got there, they had went out shopping for a little while so we went into their hotel room, then went downstairs to the pool.

My husband, sister-in-law and I were sitting on the chairs in the pool area under the umbrella, thén my husband got up and went into the pool. So then my sister-in-law followed him and went into the four feet pôol and I went and sat near the six foot pool.

Then they were telling me to go to the lower part of the pool with them because I can't swim very well.

So I stood where I was sitting and my husband started to come towards me and said to his sister "I am going to get her". I heard him, so I said to him "no you're not. " and I throw myself into the six foot water in the pool.

I can swim under the water, but if I can't stand up in the water, I panic and I will drown. So I jumped into the six foot water thinking I will swim under the water until I get to five feet and then I will stand up in the five feet of water, but it didn't happen that way.

What happened was after I jumped into the water, I swam a little and I thought I was in five feet of water, so I tried to stand up in the water but the water was over my head and I couldn't catch my breath.

I was panicking. My husband realized I needed help but he can't swim at all, and his sister was on the other side of the pool and didn't even realize what was happening, she doesn't swim either.

So at this time he started to panic. He was desperately asking everyone to help me and no one came to help. All they did was look at him, knowing I was under the water. I don't know if they didn't know how to swim or if they thought he was playing around.

Meanwhile, I am under the water looking at him in desperate need of help, I had lifted up my right hand towards my husband wishing that I can grab his hand so that he can help me get out of the water.

He was trying to tell me what to do, but I was under the water and I couldn't hear him.

At that point, I knew that I was on my own, and no one was coming to help me. All of a sudden I looked up to the beautiful blue sky and saw the small beautiful shaped clouds, you can see the clouds very clear as a picture, while I was under the water, I don't know how I did it but, I lifted myself up, got some air and swam underneath the water to safety and was able to stand in the water by miracle I saved myself.

This was so scary for me, I almost lost my life one day after my brother lost his life. This was a miracle the way God helped me, because I had panicked and at this minute after looking up at the clouds I was not panicking and Jesus guided me to safety thank Jesus.

June 14, 2019 A nail stuck in the tire disappeared

My husband had told me two days ago that there was a big nail in the front tire driver side of his car. This is the car that in 2017, my family and I had seen the Angel wings in the entire windshield in the front of the car.

I told my husband that he had to fix that tire before we go back home to Florida. This was on a Friday. We had been in New York and while in New York we had to buy a battery for the auto which was leaking acid and this car is just 2 years old, which we had bought brand new, now we have to buy a new tire, which I was upset because I wasn't expecting to spend so much money on this trip. I said to my husband ``Oh no."

Now we came down from my brother – in- laws house and my husband showed me the nail in the tire. This was a pretty big nail. Then his sister and her husband drove by and he showed it to them as well. My husband's brother – in- law wanted to take the nail out but my husband said no because the tire will empty out, so he didn't take out the nail.

Then we drove to the bank to take out money to fix the tire because they don't take credit cards for services where we were going to the flat fix in New York.

After that we decided to buy a new tire because we want to be safe going home back to Florida.

My husband decided to drop me off to see my mom and he went to buy the tire. The first tire place wanted to charge him $160. Then he went to the next tire place and he found an old friend that told him God send him there to see him. He said to my husband "Long time no see". His friend told my husband that he was going to take the nail out with no charge but, when the guy looked for the nail, he never found the nail in the tire. My husband also looked over and over again trying to find the nail and never found the nail in the tire.

The nail miracle disappeared. My husband was in shock. His friend said there's no nail in the tire. The nail was never found.

Then My husband came to me where I was visiting with my mom and my family members and told us the story and everyone was saying that's a miracle and they were all in shock looking at me strangely, and I said miracles happen all the time with us. I told them about some of my miracles that I have had. And they just stared at me and said, "Wow."

June 22, 2019 Light around the image of Jesus picture

This was on a Friday. I had stayed over my sister-in-law's house, we had breakfast, then afterwards she comes over to me with this picture of the image of Jesus Christ in her hands and says to me, " look at this picture, this picture didn't have this light around his head before." I asked her, are you sure? She replied yes, it wasn't there. She asked me, "What does that mean?" I said to her," That's a good sign because light is good, and joking with her, I said to her, and besides you have an Angel in your house so that's good", and I smiled with her. Her face was just stunned.

June 28, 2019 Pain in knees, pray and feel better.

This was on a Friday. We had just got back home from New York. We emptied out the car trunk, put some things away and afterwards went to bed. The next morning I woke up and started washing clothes, making breakfast, cleaning, putting away the rest of the things we bought back etc.

Then I went outside to do gardening. When I usually do gardening, I have to bend my knees and when I bend my knees for a long time, which gardening takes a while, my knees always swell up and I get excruciating pain which is caused by having arthritis.

After I finished the gardening, my knees where swollen and in pain. I had told my husband to put some arctic ice pain relieving gel on my knees and he did. Then I went to bed and pray to Jesus to help me feel better because I wanted to go to mass the next day and I really couldn't walk. As I laid down I started to feel better, the pain was going away and the swollen was getting better.

When I woke up the next day on Sunday my knees were as if nothing happened Thank God. He always makes me feel better right away, and I was able to go to mass and kneel down as needed all through the mass.

July 7, 2019 Aneurysm going down

Today is my sister's birthday. It's 7 am just got out of bed to text my sister happy birthday, when I see this message she had sent me.

I feel like it's my birthday how happy I got to receive this message. It was great news. She has had several aneurysm surgeries already.

She tells me that she went to the doctor and the doctor told her the aneurysm and the lump she had on her head went down. I have been praying for her for a while. She had that aneurysm for a while, and she had been told, she was going to be a vegetable after the first surgery that she had and thank God she came out of surgery well.

Now she was told by the doctor that it went down. Thank you God. My sister also thanked me for praying for her. I will always continue to pray for her and all my family always. God always makes me happy with all the miracles he always makes. I have faith that this aneurysm will disappear completely with God's help.

July 9, 2019 Pain in back goes away

This was on a Tuesday. I hadn't seen my husband's cousin in a while, which she and her husband are like brother and sister to us. That's how close we all are. We had been in New York for almost a month, when my brother passed away, RIP. and her daughter had just gotten married so she was helping her daughter move, fixing her house etc.

We had missed seeing them. So after New York we had went to my daughter's house to help her with something she needed help with and when we got back home I had texted my husband's cousin to see if she was going to be around my house that day so they can come by. She replied, if she didn't get a call that she was waiting for she will come by the house.

By 12 noon she called me and said that she was coming by. I had just gotten back from the supermarket and told her I was going to start the lasagna. When I hung up the phone, I started cooking the lasagna, as I finished putting the lasagna together they got to my house. Then I started cooking the rice and fried some plantains and put garlic bread in the oven. We ate and then conversed for several hours.

Then my son come over from work to pick up his son that we babysit for him and he had dinner. Afterwards everyone went home.

Now my husband likes to joke around saying " I feel like punching someone in the eye" meaning me. So I joke back saying " I feel like knocking someone out.

And he replied ok do it" I said ok come over here. He came over to the room and me playing with him, I tried to push him on the bed, but he was to strong I couldn't move him. So I tried something else. I jumped on him forgetting that he is older now and that I don't weigh 98 lbs. anymore more.

As I jumped on him I fell back and his back went out. Now he was in pain, his back and neck hurt. I started to rub his back and neck and felt bad for him. I said I am sorry, I was just trying to play. He said I know it's ok.

Then he asked are you ok? I replied yes. When I fell, nothing hurt me, I felt like if I fell on a cushion, meanwhile I had hit the floor. Then since I had hit the closet door with my head, my husband was checking the door to see if the door was in place.

Afterwards he laid on the floor and tried to do an exercise for his back, but it didn't work, he still had pain.

Then I was going to sleep and he tells me pray so that I can feel better. I said ok. I prayed for him and when we both woke up in the morning I asked him, how's your back? He replied good. I asked him, when your back goes out, does it get better the next day like now. He said no, thank you for praying. I said thank you God.

July 9, 2019 Conversations about Jesus

I was in conversation with my husbands cousin while she and her husband were visiting us at my house.

I had been telling her about the day that my husband and I were driving from New York and we saw the image of Jesus in the clouds.

She told me that she believes that Jesus will appear to you in the image that you will recognize that it's him, because if you would see a face of a man in the clouds, you wouldn't know who he is.

You would just say, I saw a man's face in the clouds. I said to her" yes, your right."

I believe she could be right about what she had said to me. Jesus works in mysterious ways.

July 11, 2019 I love you Jesus

I was talking to my daughter on the phone, and she tells me that she had an excruciating migraine headache.

Afterwards, she was thinking about Jesus and she said to Jesus" Jesus I love you" and the migraine headaches she had, just went away immediately.

She said that she smiled, because she knew it was Jesus that took away the pain, she felt that was his way of saying to her, he also loves her. I said to her,`" yes," that happens all the time."

We all should have faith and believe in Jesus, miracles and great things always happens to everyone. I know everyone has had a miracle but some of us haven't realized it.

Some people are always seeing lots of miracles, and if you have experienced them like me, all I say all the time is "WOW and thank you Jesus".

July 28, 2019 Arthritis Pain In Fingers

I have been writing about all my miracles and everything great that has been happening to me every day.

Today, I decided I want to write about, every night I get this pain in my index and middle fingers because of my arthritis.

These two fingers are a little swollen on the knuckles and I get pain because of it.

Tonight, I got excruciating pain in my fingers that I had to put some arctic ice pain reliever gel on my fingers, and wrap them into an ace bandage to stop the pain and to try to keep my fingers warm, because the air conditioning and ceiling fan is on in the house. And I get pain with the cold in the house, but you need it because we live in Florida and it's warm here.

I don't like taking medication, so I try to relieve the pain on my own.

I had so much pain that a asked Jesus to please take away this pain.

When I went to bed and woke up the next day, I had no pain and thank God, the pain hasn't come back as of yet.

I have realized since the swollenness has been going down.

Miracles Emailed

My husband went to the doctor and they told us he has COPD. So I called Edna and ask for prayer. After Edna's prayers the doctor took more tests and told us that the lungs were much much better. That's a miracle because they were not giving us much hope. Thank you so much for your prayers.

Felt presence of Jesus

One day, my husband and I went shopping at Aldi supermarket. When we finished shopping, as we were driving home, there was a homeless man in the corner. I never carry cash on me because I shop with credit cards, but I had a dollar so I told my husband to give it to him, with some bottled waters. I always try to have something for them, sometimes, pizza, ice cream, water etc.

When my husband gave it to him, he said thank you to my husband, and then he stuck his head in the window, on my husband's side of the car, looked at me and said to me," Thank you, God bless you."

When I looked at him, he looked like the image of Jesus as we see him in pictures. It was very strange. He didn't know that I was the one that told my husband to give it to him, but that was very strange the way he looked at me. I always wondered about that experience. We felt as if the presence of Jesus was there with us.

My Apology

I want to apologize to any person that feels offended by my true experiences. I have been a Catholic ever since I was born. I have always gone to Mass. Furthermore, I am not a miracle maker or a fortune teller. It's just that God has blessed me so much with lots of miracles, that I want to share them with the world. God loves us all, and hears all our prayers. We have all had miracles and if anyone wants to share your miracle for a future book, you can text me at blessingsmiraclesfromGod33@yahoo.com. THANK You, And God Bless You All.

Printed in the United States
By Bookmasters